In their book *Engaged Boards Will Fundraise!*, Michael Davidson and Brian Saber have provided a passport to effective governance. It is essential reading for the more than 5 million nonprofit board members who are seeking to bring their talents to bear on the greatest challenges facing our world today.

—Michael Seltzer
Distinguished Lecturer & Director
The New York Community Trust Leadership Fellows

I will be adding *Engaged Boards Will Fundraise!* to the syllabus for my signature course "Leveraging Non-Profit Boards for Organizational Success." *Engaged Boards Will Fundraise!* provides a pithy roadmap for board members et al. to succeed by exquisitely detailing the inextricable and absolutely essential link between governance and fundraising.

—Gordon J. Campbell
Professor of Practice
NYU Wagner School of Public Service

Michael Davidson and Brian Saber nailed it! This brilliant book crystalizes the direct relationship between board governance and fundraising effectiveness. A first. This is a must-read for board members and nonprofit leaders who seek authentic engagement and fundraising abundance.

—Katherine DeFoyd
Founding Partner
Growth for Good & Search for Good

Great nonprofit organizations are shepherded, guided and led by highly-effective boards. These high-impact boards are composed of fully-engaged individuals who understand their role and perform it with excellence. Unfortunately, the vast majority of new nonprofit board members don't receive even a modicum of governance training. Despite the critical role boards play in mission achievement, most nonprofits toss newly elected directors into the fray and hope they will just figure it out. I consider that to be governance malpractice.

Brian Saber and Michael Davidson are clearly on a mission to change that reality. With this book, they strengthen the social good sector by sharing their decades of experience and insights, including practical discussion guides and actionable tasks that boards can use right away to optimize performance. This powerful one-two punch of both insight and action provides a helpful roadmap for any board chair, governance committee chair, or chief executive wishing to transform governance at their organization.

—Rob Acton
Founder & CEO
Cause Strategy Partners

engaged boards *will* fundraise!

engaged boards *will* fundraise!

how good governance inspires them

michael davidson
and brian saber

Engaged Boards Will Fundraise!

Asking Matters
P.O. Box 1295
Maplewood, NJ 07040
www.askingmatters.com

This publication contains the opinions and ideas of the authors. It is intended to provide helpful and informative material on the subject matter covered. It is sold with the understanding that the authors and publisher are not engaged in rendering professional services in the book. If the reader requires personal assistance or advice, a competent professional should be consulted. The authors and publisher specifically disclaim any responsibility for any liability, loss, or risk, personal or otherwise, which is incurred as a consequence, directly or indirectly, of the use and application of any of the contents of this book. No liability is assumed for damages resulting from the use of information contained within.

Printed in the United States of America

ISBN: 978-1-7330875-6-8

Book and cover design by Thomas Edward West of Amarna Books and Media
Photograph of Brian Saber by Colleen D'Alessandro

contents

dedication

This book is is written for, and dedicated to, the nonprofit leader who knows they need their board to be more engaged in fundraising, and know that deeper engagement in true governance responsibilities is necessary to motivate that fundraising.

We dedicate this to you, the board chair, who is banging your head against the wall trying to get the board to be more enthusiastic about fundraising.

We dedicate this to you, the head of the governance committee, who is trying to figure out what structures and responsibilities to develop to better engage the board and to help it understand its fundraising role and feel committed to helping.

We dedicate this to you, the board member who wants to do your best job and needs to learn what it takes.

We dedicate this to you, the executive director or CEO, who is trying to give your board leadership guidance and support, and needs the board to better understand their role if they're going to partner with you effectively to build the organization's resources.

We dedicate this to you, the director of development, who can't open important doors on your own, and can't cultivate, steward, and solicit all the worthwhile prospects without the board's help.

about the authors

 I'm **Michael Davidson**, president of Board Coach. I started my career as an anthropologist and a lawyer, but I decided 30 years back to use my legal skills and understanding of process and group dynamics to help the nonprofit sector improve the way boards govern. I've now worked with the boards of well over 150 organizations. Among my other work, I was the lead trainer and curriculum designer for the United Way Board Serve program, which is designed to teach up-and-coming leaders the ins and outs of board leadership. I am currently leading a master class for experienced consultants to enable them to assist their nonprofit clients with their board management issues. www.boardcoach.com

 I'm **Brian Saber**, president of Asking Matters. I jumped into the nonprofit world right out of college and worked in nonprofits for 25 years as the head fundraiser or executive director. In 2008, I felt I could help the field more by teaching everything I've learned about asking individuals for gifts, and I've been doing that for the last 13 years. In addition to the thousands of nonprofits that benefit from Asking Matters memberships, webinars, courses, and other products, I train boards and staff around the country, lead sessions and deliver keynotes at conferences, and coach and consult with numerous organizations. I am also the author of two other books, *Asking Styles: Revolutionize Your Fundraising* and *Boards and Asking Styles: A Roadmap to Success*. www.askingmatters.com

our unique collaboration

We've now known each other for 20 years, having first met through Hudson Guild, where Michael was the board governance consultant and Brian was Associate Executive Director for External Relations.

Over the years we've led trainings together, worked side-by-side for the same clients, developed an online course together, and leaned on each other for counsel. We've also become friends and a mutual admiration society.

Through our partnership, we've not only learned a ton about each other's expertise, but we've figured out, down to the individual task, how board governance and fundraising go hand in hand. Even in the writing of this book, we had rich discussions that impacted what we recommend and how we explain the rationale for the work.

Now, as Brian leads board fundraising trainings around the country, he does so with a deep understanding of why strong governance is essential to board fundraising.

And Michael, as he consults with clients, does so with a deep understanding of the board's role in fundraising and how that impacts board structure, recruitment, job descriptions and more.

We're excited to share what we've learned with you.

why this book

Your organization—and every organization—needs its board to fundraise if it's going to fulfill its mission and make the biggest impact possible. However, motivating the board to fundraise effectively is quite possibly the most difficult work you and your fellow staff and volunteer leaders have on your plate.

Board members must have a deep personal connection with the vision, mission, and values of the organization, and they must see themselves as members of a team that has responsibility for governing and guiding the organization toward the achievement of that mission.

Most board members, however, have very little experience with fundraising, and if they do, it often consists of "hitting up" those they know…and then having to make reciprocal gifts. Thinking this is what's expected, board members will say "I'll do anything but fundraise," or "I hate fundraising and can't do it." Sound familiar?

Under duress, your board members will try their best at this "quid-pro-quo" fundraising, hating it along the way and getting burnt out. Sooner than later they'll say, "I just don't have anyone else to ask."

Our goal is to get your board involved in a strategic way, where they are partnering to build long-term resources for your organization, rather than bringing in transactional gifts which end up being a short-term solution.

Engaged Boards Will Fundraise! is based on the following proposition:

> Much has been written about the importance of board engagement in fundraising and much has been written about the importance of good governance. Yet the two topics are often addressed separately.
>
> We believe they must be addressed together as it is only when your Board is actively engaged in its role in the governance, leadership and oversight of the organization that it will have the tools and motivation to actively engage in fundraising for your organization.

And the money is out there for the asking!

In 2020, $471 billion in charitable gifts was given in the U.S. What percentage do you think came from individuals?

Most people don't realize that 68.8% of all charitable dollars came from outright gifts from individuals, and another 8.8% in bequests, which are also from individuals. In addition, half of all foundation gifts come from individual or small family foundations where an individual, couple, or family is making the decision about their money. When we add those in, 87% of all charitable gifts come from individuals.

2020 charitable giving

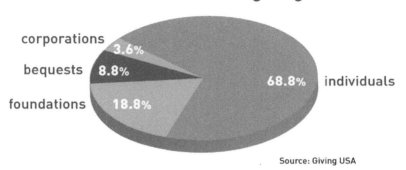

Source: Giving USA

And we know the biggest individual gifts come from cultivating and soliciting donors one-to-one. How many $10,000 gifts come from direct mail? Phone-a-thons? Even special events?

So, the question is: Which piece of the pie do you want? Obviously, the biggest part — and without your board members' deep commitment and help, you can't fully access it.

Yet most board members are not actively engaged in fundraising and don't have the proper level of responsibility for it. This holds nonprofits back in critical ways.

To address this problem, in *Engaged Boards Will Fundraise!* we will provide you with:

- an understanding of the relationship between overall board governance and fundraising;
- strategies that are most likely to motivate and engage your board in fundraising; and
- practices that can support board fundraising.

one

---

why boards?

Any discussion of the role of your board in fundraising needs to be based on an understanding of why we need to have boards in the first place. Why can't the organization just be run by your staff?

To answer this, let's look at why for-profit corporations must have boards of directors in addition to staff.

In a for-profit corporation, the legal responsibility of the board is to represent the interests of the stakeholders—in this case, the shareholders, whose interests may be different from those of management. Management, for example, might see the mission of the corporation in terms of maximizing short-term profits, while the shareholders might be more concerned with long-term growth (or vice versa).

In a nonprofit organization, the picture is more complex. Achieving the mission of your organization requires taking into account multiple stakeholders, each of whose support is necessary for the achievement of the mission, and whose views on success will differ.

Stakeholders include clients or participants, donors, community members, government funders and officers, and staff and volunteers, among others. It's the responsibility of your board to consider these different interests as it makes decisions about the direction and sustainability of the organization. And to be able to consider these interests, board members need to know what they are.

This requires your board members to meet the various stakeholders, in order to learn from them. Remember: staff and management are stakeholders themselves, and their reporting on the interests of other stakeholders may be filtered through their own interests. A good part of the work of the board has to take place away from the board table and out in the community, in person— visiting programs, talking to clients and staff, accompanying staff on meetings with funders, attending community meetings, and more.

It also requires that board membership include people whose life experiences can bring a diversity of perspectives into the conversation.

An added benefit of this aspect of in-person board engagement is that exposure to different views about the importance of the organization will deepen your members' own commitment and, with that, their motivation to engage in the fundraising work to assure success and sustainability.

- In what percentage of your board meetings have you gotten feedback directly from any stakeholders on how they view the organization?
- What percentage of your board membership can bring the diversity of perspectives needed for a full understanding of the interests and needs of your stakeholders?

NOTE:

Throughout the book we will pose questions such as these, which you can not only ask yourselves but use to frame discussions at board meetings, in committee meetings, and during strategy sessions.

---

the nonprofit difference

This perspective of multiple stakeholders has important implications for the nonprofit decision-making process.

Michael has noted over the years that a frequent complaint from board members who have corporate experience is that nonprofits spend too much time talking about issues before making a decision. Nonprofits, they complain, should act more like businesses and make decisions more quickly, and with less talk.

The fact is, nonprofits are not poorly run businesses; they are a different kind of business.

Since the criterion for a good decision in a for-profit business is whether it will serve the interest of its shareholders—i.e., make a profit—that question can be answered with data. The criterion for a good decision in a nonprofit is whether it will meet the needs of the organization's multiple stakeholders. This is not a question that can be answered simply with financial or marketing data. It requires deliberation and analysis from many different perspectives.

Let's use the example of rolling out a new product or service for children. A nonprofit will ask: Does the staff have the capacity, and do they want to do it? What do the kids think about it? Their parents? Is the community going to be up in arms about this? These kinds of questions aren't all answerable by data—they're often judgments based on people's perceptions.

We must always remember that the government agrees to incorporate us as nonprofits with the understanding that our goal is one of doing good, and it expects each board to be the gatekeeper assuring that an organization is, in fact, doing good. If the board is not in touch with stakeholders and doesn't have a rich understanding of what they need, it can't possibly govern properly and make decisions in their best interests.

So while it's true that your board members won't be motivated to fundraise if they aren't fully invested in your organization, it's also true that your board members can't be good governors without being fully invested. Rubber stamps don't govern well—and they certainly don't fundraise well.

two

---

the evolution
of boards

Many of the challenges in getting your board to fundraise are due to the disconnect between how your organization has evolved and grown, and how much your board has evolved and grown to meet the organization's current needs. What do we mean by that?

In the broadest terms, most organizations start with a visionary who has an idea and gathers their friends, relatives, and peers to form a board. Everyone does whatever needs to be done. Mostly that's hands-on work, as new organizations often have no paid staff. And when it comes to fundraising, everyone pitches in on low-cost fundraisers, asking everyone they know to attend and doing the hands-on work to make the events happen.

As organizations mature, they hire professional staff to do the work the volunteers used to do, and the board's role turns more to governing. At this point, the board's fundraising role also needs to change. However, these changes don't always happen at the same time. In fact, the board is often playing catch-up, as it's more likely to react in response to the new needs than to evolve in advance to anticipate those needs.

Because organizations are always in transition along this spectrum, there needs to be an explicit understanding on the part of your board about where they are located as that transition happens. Their understanding of this will strongly affect their view of the appropriate balance between hands-on support—which might have been very important at the organization's founding stage—and current needs for fiduciary oversight, strategic and policy leadership, and fundraising.

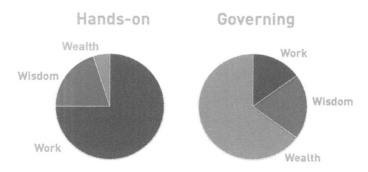

The need for "Work, Wisdom, and Wealth," as we often say in our industry, is present at every stage of your organization's evolution. However, the balance between those components will change, most importantly with respect to the amount of time and energy devoted to wealth (personal giving and fundraising) rather than hands-on support. Let's explore how this balance affects the way your board operates, how your board is composed, and what its fundraising role is.

board operations

In the early years, a board is dedicated to supporting a founding leader or group. Board members do anything and everything to keep the organization going, and they make decisions together.

Hands-on   **Governing**

- supports a founding leader or group
- does everything
- committee of the whole

- more of the management role shifts to ED/staff
- board relies on the ED for financial management and programmatic leadership
- division of labor into committees

In a mature organization, the staff makes the day-to-day decisions, and the board relies on the staff to manage the finances and the programs. The board's work is now done in committees.

board composition

As we noted earlier, the founding board is often comprised of friends and family of the founder who serve as a "band of warriors" supporting that founder. There's usually some commitment to the mission, but a much stronger commitment to the founder.

Hands-on   **Governing**

- friends & family
- "band of warriors"
- strong personal commitment to the founder

- broad range of professionals with specific talents
- greater diversity
- large donors
- strong personal commitment to the mission

fundraising

Founding boards are kept busy bringing in small dollars wherever they can. They cast the net wide. Often, they are giving of their time but not their wallets—and if they are giving, they are not giving their largest gifts.

Hands-on   **Governing**

- ask everyone you know for help
- run numerous small fundraising events
- may or may not give personal gifts

- provide fundraising oversight
- make significant gifts
- cultivate and solicit major donors

On a more mature board, fundraising is done more strategically. The board provides oversight, contributes personally, is asked to identify others who might join the cause, and is asked to assist staff in the cultivation (and solicitation) of donors. Board members are also asked to make more significant personal gifts.

ACTIVITY: Where in the evolution between hands-on and governing are you?

- Have everyone, individually, mark on a flipchart where they see the organization in each of the three areas: board operations, board composition, and fundraising.
- Compare results and discuss:
  - ◇ Is everyone in agreement as to where you are?
  - ◇ Do you find you're at different points in operations, composition, and fundraising?
  - ◇ Overall, where do you think you should be, and what are the greatest challenges you see to getting there?

Do you find variations in where you are in each area? To the extent that your board may be lagging in one or more of these areas, it's important to begin a process to better align your board members among themselves and with your organization.

You can expect resistance to change, with board members expressing:

"But that's not the way we've always done it."

"This is our culture."

"Why do we need to change?"

A conversation around these questions might be a good start:

- What work that the board has been doing is no longer needed?
- What matters that the board has been discussing should be left to staff?

- What are the areas where more board attention is needed?
- What work has the board *not* been doing that is now needed?

So, how do you move your board ahead if it's not where you need it to be?

Brian likes to say you've got two options—revolution and evolution.

With revolution, you throw the baby out with the bathwater and start all over again—in this case, with a new board. That's an extreme and fraught solution only to be used in extreme cases where a board is truly dysfunctional and, possibly, malfeasant.

Most often, evolution is the way to go. If you make a plan to address everything we discuss, and you genuinely engage the board in the process, in a year you'll find your board has made significant progress. Within three years your board will be transformed and will be a powerful fundraising partner.

Keep in mind: Over those three years numerous new board members will have joined, many current board members will have grown in their roles, and a few might have left because they don't think they fit in with the new expectations. You might still have a few old-timers who neither grow nor leave, but they will be in the minority and their opinions will not dictate board activity.

three

---

what motivates
board service
individually?

As an organization grows, the need for oversight becomes more complex and involves mission questions and policies around growth, program impact, strategic direction, financial scenarios, and the like. By custom and practice, we also add more significant fundraising expectations.

These expectations will, however, remain a formality unless your board members—who are, after all, volunteers—are motivated to live up to them. So, what motivates board service?

Think for a minute of what you ask of your board members.

First: "Please attend a number of board meetings—probably in the evening when you'd rather be relaxing. Oh, and they may or may not be interesting!"

Second: "If you're looking to use up more of your evening time, we have good news for you. We'll ask you to sit on at least one committee and it will probably meet at night—or we'll want to Zoom while you're trying to get your work done during the day."

But wait, there's more! "We'll ask you to make a significant contribution of dollars for the honor of attending those meetings (and having lots of governance/fiduciary responsibility)."

And here's the kicker. "To top it off we'll ask you to help us fundraise."

"Should we sign you up now, before the mad rush?"

Obviously, once your organization is past the founding period—where board members are there because of their relationship to the founder—there needs to be a great personal reward to undertaking this role, right?

We believe there are three general areas of reward:
- Coming with and maintaining a deep personal concern for the achievement of the mission
- The personal satisfaction of making an impact
- Having the experience of being part of an effective and supportive group

To what extent do you think your board members experience these rewards? How are you doing in providing them?

If you're like most boards, you've got some work to do here. For your board members to fully reap these rewards and make the biggest impact they can, you must develop a culture that motivates the full engagement of each of them, individually and collectively.

We'll discuss deep personal concern and making an impact

in this chapter, as both can be achieved individually to some extent. Then we'll talk about effective and supportive groups in Chapter 4, as they are necessary to maximize impact individually and collectively.

deep personal concern

We strongly believe your board members should come to your organization with a deep personal concern for the challenges that your organization is addressing, and with agreement as to your vision for the world and how accomplishing your mission will make that vision a reality. We'll talk a bit more about this in Chapter 9 when we talk about recruitment.

That personal concern for, and belief in, your organization must be continually reinforced through direct contact with the cause, or you risk your board members acting in a vacuum and without their personal compass. How do you maintain that contact?

First, it's critically important to strengthen the mission connection for individual board members. Based on our experience, we recommend each of your board members visit/experience programs at least twice, and preferably three times, annually. Given the general newfound comfort with video conferencing, board members should be able to experience programs even more often than that (with an exception for programs that have privacy and legal restrictions).

After experiencing programs, they should come back and report to their fellow board members what they experienced and learned on their visits.

- Currently, how often do your board members visit/experience programs, on average?

- How often do board members report to the board on what they've learned?
- Would your board agree to the expectation that they visit/experience programs at least twice a year?

Not only do your board members need to report back, but they need to hear mission stories from staff and clients. And there needs to be a discussion at board meetings as to the significance of these stories and how to use them in fundraising.

- At what percentage of board meetings is there is a meaningful story presented by staff or clients?

making an impact

Though your board members were attracted to your organization because of their deep personal concern for the cause and for the impact your organization can have on the world, they may find themselves spending the bulk of their time on fiduciary matters such as budget, infrastructure, resources...and very little time on questions of direction and mission impact.

While infrastructure is obviously of great importance, engaging them in questions of strategy and mission impact will strengthen their motivation in different ways. Is your board wrestling with questions about your long-range sustainability? Or whether you're representing your constituents well? Or building staff leadership? Or measuring outcomes correctly? Remember, engaged boards will fundraise!

- What percentage of your board meetings is spent on questions of organizational direction and mission impact?

Staff can tend to see these questions as within their purview and engage the board on them as little as possible. But to the extent that the board is not engaged in questions of mission direction and impact and sees them as the responsibility of staff, they will tend to see staff as having sole responsibility for the viability and sustainability of the organization as well.

Therefore, it is important to engage the board in these questions at the appropriate level. For instance, "What impact are we trying to have? "How will we measure the impact so we know we're fulfilling our mission?" and "Who should we be serving?" We will talk more about this in the next chapter.

- What topics sparked the most engaging conversations your board had this past year? Are there similar conversations you can have going forward?

As you now can see, building a cohesive, committed board takes a good deal of effort and, for many boards, a significant change to their way of doing business. If you want engaged board members willing to contribute generously and develop the organization's resources, they need to be empowered appropriately.

four

what motivates board service collectively?

effective and supportive groups

The third motivating reward for board members is being part of an effective and supportive group. It is probably one of the few universal truths of human behavior that as a species we are at our best when we are working as part of a group. And when we are at our best because we're working as part of an effective group, we make a bigger impact overall, and that enhances our personal reward. It also keeps deep personal concern, our North Star, at the fore.

While group identification can, of course, have negative con-
sequences—such as when it leads to war or social injustice—it is
also our evolutionary advantage as a species.

There are innumerable examples of the power of teams. The
oft-heard line in soldiers' writings is that the most important thing
for them was to bring their team home safely. We see this team
dynamic in Olympic athletes with better times in relay events than
in individual events. Michael is a rower, so he thinks of the motivating call from the coxswain—"We are the USA women's eight!"—
that moved the 2016 American women's crew from second place
to first.

The job of leadership is to create the structures to transform a
board into a team.

We can each recall groups that we've been members of that
powerfully engaged our commitment, loyalty, and energy, such as
sports teams, neighborhood coalitions, project teams, and reli-

gious communities. What are the qualities that transformed each of those collections of individuals into an effective group?

We believe there are six attributes of effective and supportive groups:

1. Goals that are clear, impactful, and agreed-to
2. Clear expectations for each board member
3. Trust that all board members are living up to expectations
4. Dynamic and open discussion
5. Leadership that assures respectful communication, transparency, and respect for time
6. Collegiality and fun

Let's look at each of the attributes individually.

goals that are clear, impactful, and agreed-to

To begin with, it is important to have clarity on the process by which goals are set. Your board must be engaged in that process. If they're not, you can't expect their commitment and engagement to the achievement of the goals. Nor can you expect their commitment to raising the funds needed to achieve the goals. Engaged boards will fundraise!

Goals are often set at an annual meeting or planning retreat. The retreat—and any goal-setting—starts with the staff presenting opportunities and challenges for the next year, after which the board discusses them. The board and staff then together agree to priorities, and the board agrees to its role by identifying specific committee deliverables that will lead to the achievement of the agreed-upon goals.

Of course, goals will inevitably need to be changed or modified as the year progresses. Just be sure your board is made explicitly aware of any changes and can discuss and agree to any that are significant.

- Do you have an annual board/staff goal-setting retreat?
- If not, what is your process for determining organizational and board action priorities?

clear expectations

Boards work best when board members know what is expected of them and are confident that all their fellow team members are living up to the same expectations.

"I can't do my job if I don't know what it is and I won't do it if I'm not sure my teammates are doing theirs as well."

In another of Michael's rowing analogies, in *The Boys in the Boat* the coach says, "You will be the best rower you can be when you trust your teammates."

NOTE:

Throughout the book, we will reference helpful materials we're making available to you at:

askingmatters.com/boardresources

You'll find sample expectations there.

There are two categories of expectations: measurable expectations and agreed-to cultural norms.

Measurable expectations are those that could be reported back to your board members and to the governance committee in a "report card." They include board meeting attendance, commit-tee participation, committee or board leadership, personal con-tributions, and fundraising involvement. Which of the following five measurable expectations would your board agree to?

- Attend all board meetings
- Serve as an active member of a committee
- Be willing, if asked, to accept a committee or board leader-ship position
- Make a "personally significant" financial contribution
- Use their best efforts to recruit financial and other resources

In addition to these measurable expectations, there are cultur-al norms that are equally important. These norms include:

- Respect for fellow board members and the work they do in their committees
- Readiness to check one's ego at the door—to say "it's not about me"
- Willingness to listen to and consider perspectives different from their own
- Respect for the dedication and work of the staff
- Provision of helpful refinements rather than outright revis-ing others' work

While these norms are common sense, making them explicit and agreeing to them provides great support for your chair or another board member when a board meeting—or a board mem-ber—seems to be going off the rails.

Respect for committee work is of crucial importance. While we want board members to actively engage in critical mat-ters, to the extent that they react to committee recommen-dations by wordsmithing or re-opening issues completely, it disempowers the committees. Board members can, of course, make helpful suggestions, but the approach should be to accept the recommendations unless doing so clearly creates a significant risk.

- Thinking back on all the expectations we've discussed, would your board agree to them?

trust that all board members are living up to expectations

We all know that expectations are only of value to the extent that they're understood and agreed to. We would never just give a person that we supervise a job description without following up. The work gets done only if there are periodic supervisory meetings.

Using an assessment tool we're providing at askingmatters. com/boardresources, or another assessment template that you have, schedule an annual individual self-assessment and conversation with appropriate board leadership to review accomplishments, problem-solve, and set personal development goals and action objectives.

It is important that this process include an exploration of how the board experience can be valuable to the board member:

- What skills would you like to develop?
- What might you like to learn or experience? How can we help?
- What would make next year better for you?

Do you have an assessment process? If yes, what is it? If no, why not?

dynamic and open discussion

As we noted in the previous chapter, board members must feel they are making an impact. Some of the impact they make is through individual efforts, but much of a board member's time is spent in board meetings. As we will discuss in the next chapter, it is through the outcomes of those meetings that members make much of their impact.

Given this, the time spent in board meetings should be a time when you engage the thinking of board members in analysis of issues of strategic importance. It should not be a time for updating or routine reporting, as there are alternative ways to provide information.

Board members can read—they don't need to be read to. Therefore, board meetings should have timed consent agendas, and board members should agree to a practice where routine reports will be provided in advance and will not be discussed unless a board member sends a specific question in advance of the meeting. Board members come to you because they want to utilize their critical and creative facilities on behalf of your mission, not to be collectors of operational and other detail.

This will leave time for significant agenda topics that deal with fiduciary oversight and with generative and strategic consideration of the direction and growth of the organization. It is important that new ideas on other topics, which may come up, are not discussed without having those ideas first referred to committees.

- What percentage of your board meetings is spent giving reports vs. spent in discussion?

Board meetings should also have brief executive sessions. An executive session is a device many boards adopt to promote open discussion. Coming at the end of the meeting, it can be as brief as 10 minutes. The session is for reflection on the meeting and has no agenda and no minutes.

It allows for the expression of ideas that board members may have had during the meeting but self-censored due to the presence of staff. It allows for the symbolic reinforcement of the board as a body in itself and as the body legally responsible for the organization. Should issues arise that require broader discussion, the chair will be able to communicate that to the executive director.

leadership that assures respectful communication, transparency, and respect for time

Whose job is it to make sure that meetings are engaging and productive? It's your board chair's. In fact, this is one of their key roles.

The board chair needs to be sure that there's a mechanism for giving each board member feedback on their job, and must engage and support each board member. The board chair must keep the big picture in mind at all times, and promote open and respectful discussion at board meetings.

Whose job is it to provide feedback to the chair on their performance? The executive director. Although the executive director reports to the board generally, and to the chair on a day-to-day basis, there needs to be a trusting and open dialogue between them that goes both ways.

collegiality and fun

Teams become stronger to the extent that team members know each other personally, understand each other's passion for the mission, and, hopefully, are collegial with each other. By collegial we don't mean that they socialize independently, but that at a minimum, they interact socially through board interactions, know personal things about each other, and have had an opportunity to learn about each other's passion for the mission.

To the extent that board members know one another personally, they are more likely to want to come to board meetings, work hard so that they don't disappoint their colleagues, and engage in mutually respectful discussion...even when they disagree.

- How collegial do you think your board is?

- How many board members do each of your board members know personally—at least somewhat?

- Do you create informal opportunities for socialization among your board members, such as a glass of wine after a meeting, an annual board dinner, etc.?

- Do you help organize or encourage one-on-one conversations among board members?

At the board retreat or meeting, divide the board into small groups to develop recommendations to address a specific issue. In addition to generating helpful ideas, this will serve to connect board members with one another and to give each member an opportunity to participate.

TEAM BUILDING EXERCISES

Michael has used the following simple exercises to build effective teams and create a culture of engagement:

- Prior to a board retreat or meeting, assign pairs of board members to interview each other about who they are and what aspect of the mission is most important to them. At the retreat, have them introduce each other.

- At the board retreat or meeting, divide the board into small groups to develop recommendations to address a specific issue. In addition to generating helpful ideas, this will serve to connect board members with one another and to give each member an opportunity to participate.

five

---

board
responsibilities

Let's now discuss your board's responsibilities to your organization, and how fulfilling these responsibilities strengthens the board's fundraising engagement and capacity.

The fiduciary responsibility of your board to the mission, and to the interests of its stakeholders, is legally defined in three specific duties. They are the duties of care, loyalty, and obedience. Let's discuss each of them.

duty of care

It is the responsibility of board members to be reasonably informed, participate in the decisions of the board, and act in good faith, which means using the same care that an ordinarily prudent person would use in similar circumstances.

Fulfilling this duty is necessary to position your board members to be able to help fundraise (and develop other resources). For example, a board member who doesn't prepare for a board meeting by reading the materials, or who is absent from or unengaged in the discussion, won't be in a position to convincingly represent your organization.

duty of loyalty

This means acting in the best interests of the organization, disclosing any personal interests, not voting in those instances, and avoiding even the appearance of a conflict of interest. In addition to assuring that board decision-making is based on the interests of the organization and not individual self-interest, it is impossible for board members to honestly solicit contributions if they are personally benefitting from them.

duty of obedience

While legal compliance is fairly straightforward, obedience to the mission is more complex because of the different interests of the many different stakeholders.

Engagement in questions about the extent to which programs are effectively achieving the mission is central to the process of building a truly engaged board, and also to enabling board members to convincingly speak about the impact the organization is having. For a youth-serving organization, for example, what are the social and emotional learning objectives and how are they measured?

- What are two recent examples of board discussions you've had about effective mission impact? If you can't think of any in the last year, this should be an indication that your board might not be engaged enough to be effective fund-raisers.

Another way to look at these duties is to understand that they fall into two distinct categories and are fulfilled in different ways:

Resource development, while it requires everyone's participation, is accomplished by your board members individually. But legislative, oversight, and fiduciary responsibilities are accomplished only by your board as a whole, acting as a legal decision-making body.

legislative, oversight, and fiduciary responsibilities

On the legislative/oversight/fiduciary side, boards have five responsibilities. They are:

- Provide financial oversight
- Set policy and establish strategic decisions
- Assure there are adequate resources

- Maintain themselves as a cohesive and committed board
- Select, support, partner, and evaluate the executive director

provide financial oversight

The board's first priority is assuring the fiscal health of the organization. This means regular reviews of the financials to ensure that the organization is on solid footing, establishing financial controls, and developing scenarios for financial sustainability under different eventualities.

The development of the budget requires special attention. The budget process is an opportunity for your board and staff to engage in a thoughtful planning process. Should the budget be a replica of the prior year? Are there new infrastructure and programmatic needs that should be addressed?

The process of approving the budget is similarly important—an opportunity to train your board in understanding the financial structure of the organization. Active involvement in this process will help board members make the case to potential donors about the need for resources and how their gifts will lead to fulfilling the organization's vision and making the biggest impact.

For organizations with endowments or other investment or reserve accounts, the board must create an investment policy.

set policy and establish strategic decisions

The board must establish organizational values and personnel policies, identify who is being served, and identify the impact the organization wants to have. Working on these issues will sharpen the board's understanding of the organization, deepen their sense of ownership, and increase their confidence in engaging others to invest in it. While the final decision in these areas is a board responsibility, the proposals will always be developed in collaboration with staff.

- Where do you think your board is on this front?

assure there are adequate resources

The board, starting with the Finance and Program Committees, should be looking at the question of what is meant by "adequate" resources. Of course, adequate can mean many things, from providing what was provided last year, to providing enough to enhance programs, to providing enough to grow towards significant mission achievement.

maintain a cohesive and committed board

Maintaining a cohesive and committed board involves recruiting the right people, orienting them properly, reviewing their performance, and developing policies that ensure you retain them. Each element of this process should be viewed as an opportunity to create the board that the organization needs, and to evolve the board as the needs of the organization evolve.

Recruitment of new members and retention of current members must be looked at as opportunities to achieve the qualities the organization needs in its board: appropriate skills, team cohesion, access to resources, and diversity/equity/inclusion. We will discuss recruitment and retention in Chapter 9.

select, support, and partner with the executive director

While boards are very diligent when hiring an executive director, the task of supporting, partnering with, and reviewing the executive director often falls short. The annual review is of particular importance because board members frequently do not know what the executive director actually does or, worse, each member has a different idea.

The review, based on a self-assessment and a board and staff survey, is a way to get everyone on the same page and to clarify, of necessity, the work of the board and the work of the partnership between board and staff. It can also strengthen the partnership between the board and the executive director by clarifying mutual expectations.

six

decision-making

Your board members need to understand where their role ends and the staff's role begins. That can be difficult, as almost every area of governance responsibility intersects with a management responsibility.

Unless these overlaps are looked at explicitly, there is the continual danger of different and conflicting understandings, creating a scenario where your board feels excluded and your staff, at the same time, feel intruded upon. When your board feels that it's being excluded, it will, subconsciously, move the resource development responsibility to your staff.

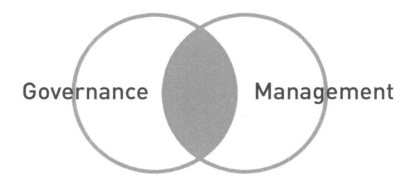

Here are some common examples of the intersection between staff and board spheres of authority:

- Staff must develop the budget and then present it to the board for review and approval.
- Staff must recommend—and, of course, implement—programs, but the board must conduct the litmus test. Will the new program advance the mission? Is it worth the additional resources?
- And while staff are supervised by the executive director or another manager, the board must make sure that the appropriate personnel policies exist and that they are followed.

There are two distinct ways to clearly distinguish responsibilities:

- Adopt official policies to distinguish governance roles from management roles.
- Utilize operational criteria to guide specific decisions about whether a question is for the board or staff. These deci-

sions are usually made jointly by the executive director and the chair and/or the executive committee.

official policies

This is the Carver Policy Approach, developed by John Carver in 1990.[1] His approach very broadly delegates authority to the staff through the executive director, who is directed to achieve certain results within certain parameters. The board sets up policies that limit the latitude the executive director has.

The Carver Approach has been used principally by elected boards such as school boards, town councils, etc. It is useful, however, as a general statement of principles.

operational criteria

This approach involves agreeing on the factors that should determine who makes the decision:

1. Does it fall within an area of board responsibility for oversight, fiscal sustainability, or policy, such as budget approval, policy approval, strategic directions, etc.?
2. To what extent does the decision involve "significant" risk to the assets or reputation of the organization? The greater the risk, the more likely the board should be involved. A new office lease is more likely to be a board decision than a new copier lease.
3. Who has the best information with which to make the de-

---

[1] Carver, J. (1990). Boards That Make A Difference: A New Design for Leadership in Nonprofit and Public Organizations. San Francisco, CA: Jossey-Bass (2nd edition, 1997; 3rd edition, 2006).

cision? Choosing an architect and designing the office lay-
out requires detailed knowledge of operations that board
members cannot be expected to have.

4. What is the organizational impact of who decides? To the
extent the board becomes directly involved in hiring or personnel decisions, this can undermine the authority of the
executive director. For example, the board may approve an
amount recommended by the executive director for a one-
time bonus for staff but should not attempt to dictate the
amounts allocated to each staff member.

For executive directors concerned about the board microman-
aging, it is important to remember that the level of information
that the executive director provides to the board will impact their
view of their sphere of decision-making. If, for example, the executive director provides operational detail in reporting to the
board, board members will assume these are matters for their
input and decision-making.

Information that might be "nice to know" could be sent by
email or posted in an online portal. The information presented
at a board meeting should only be that which board members
"need to know" or "need to approve". If the board should not be
spending its meeting digging into operational detail, that detail
should not be placed on the table.

It's important to be clear that the authority we've been talking
about is the authority of the board as the whole, and not the
authority of individual board members. Board members wear
a "governance hat" only when attending board meetings where
they act collectively. On their own, they have no authority.

For instance, the chair of the Program Committee may bring
a recommendation to the board about the impact objectives of

a program, but that chair cannot direct staff to change how they are working with clients. The Marketing Committee may recommend a strategy for reaching a specific audience. A member of the committee helping the staff to design a brochure is, however, wearing a "volunteer hat" in that role—assisting but not directing the staff member.

- Do you think your board understands the distinction between the governance areas they're responsible for and the management areas that are the purview of the staff?

seven

---

managing the division of labor

In creating the engagement and commitment that helps board members succeed at fundraising, understanding the principles underlying the work of the board is only the first step. Like all principles, they are only as useful as they are well-managed. And part of managing the work of the board is dividing the labor.

There are three structures that can facilitate the management of the division of labor: a board management team, weekly meetings between your board chair and executive director, and an annual board retreat.

board management team

First, there must be some group of board members who manage your board. In most boards that could be your Executive Committee, but it can equally well just be your chair, one other officer, and your executive director, making up a less formal board management team. Some organizations have used a management team composed of the chairs of the key committees. This enables smoother coordination of the work of those committees.

This management team meets in between board meetings. So, what should this committee do—and not do?

- It should plan for and manage your board's activity.
- It should oversee and coordinate the work of the committees. Are they moving ahead? Are they keeping to their mission?
- It should develop the agenda for your board meetings, including whether a matter is for board decision, board input, or information purposes only.
- Finally, it should support and evaluate your executive director. This can also be done separately by an ad hoc task force.
- It should not make legal decisions except for time-sensitive emergency issues.
- It should not "become the board."

If your management team is your Executive Committee, which has certain emergency decision-making authority, it should only use this authority in narrow circumstances. Often those circumstances have to do with time constraints.

But you must always ask yourself: "Is it imperative that this decision be made now by this body?" Because the more often this committee makes decisions, the less empowered, and therefore less engaged and less committed, the rest of your board will be.

Further, your executive director must bring the appropriate material to the Executive Committee (or the board, for that matter). While it is important to think about what not to share, such as operational detail, it is equally important to think about what to share.

Executive directors need to work towards a relationship with their board where they are comfortable sharing significant concerns in a way that will lead to a constructive engagement in problem-solving. For your Executive Committee, and board members generally, to see themselves as true partners with your executive director, they must be given the bad news as well as the good. This engagement will strengthen the board's commitment to fundraising. (You can probably hear us saying "Engaged boards *will* fundraise!" in your head at this point!)

weekly chair/executive director meetings

The second structure to put in place is a weekly meeting between your board chair and executive director. This should be for a frank discussion of any organizational issues and how the board might be productively involved. It is also an opportunity to sort out details of the board/management interface such as requests from board members for information from staff, etc.

These weekly meetings (or bi-weekly for small organizations) are also an opportunity to build and sustain a collaborative and mutually supportive partnership and, interestingly, to provide mutual coaching and mentoring. Your executive director can offer professional experience in helping your chair manage the board, effectively facilitate meetings, address the needs of specific board members, and the like. Similarly, your chair, who may have deep business or management experience, can provide that guidance.

- How often each month, on average, do your chair and executive director meet?

annual board retreat

Annual board planning retreats are a management tool and facilitate making a meaningful allocation of work between the board and staff so that you're maximizing each—and taking into account the realistic capacities of the two. You should emerge from the retreat with a plan for accomplishing your objectives in the year ahead.

The retreat needs to be organized around a staff presentation of current challenges and opportunities and a discussion of the role of each committee in addressing them. This plan will, of course, need to be adjusted as you go along, but it should include clear objectives for the board as well as for the staff. Your board objectives will include specific deliverables for each committee, to be monitored by your board management team.

This process ensures that board members feel they are integrally involved in moving the organization forward, and that they are aware of how the strategy will unfold so that they can be knowledgeable and articulate cultivators and solicitors of donors.

eight

---

basic committee
functions

Solid committee structures maximize the efficiency of board operations, and this efficiency can help to deepen board member commitment as they see that their time is valued and well spent. It can also optimize the time available for fundraising.

Keep in mind that your board members, however committed, only have so much time to devote to their role. If their work in committees is inefficient, it will not only be uninspiring, but it will take up the time you'd like them to devote to helping you cultivate and solicit individual gifts.

Further, if your board committees aren't high functioning, their work will need to be addressed at board meetings. We've already talked about the need for board meetings to be focused on strategic issues. That won't happen if your committees are not working correctly.

The five basic committees of the board are:

- Finance/Audit
- Resource Development
- Board Development/Governance
- Program Planning
- Executive

There may, of course, be other committees or task forces that a board may need, such as Marketing, Real Estate, Investment, etc.

For a small board, these committees might have as few as two people and you're likely to have a non-board member or two on them as well. On particularly small boards you may even combine functions such as Executive and Governance.

During the founding/start-up phase, boards often work on these separate functions as a "committee of the whole" where all topics are worked on at board meetings. This may seem simpler, but it's exhausting and inefficient. Most importantly, much will fall through the cracks as boards focus on the crisis of the day. Therefore, even on young and small boards, we recommend dividing out the work among committees.

finance/audit

The Finance/Audit Committee has three roles.

The first is to approve your annual budget and monitor it throughout the year. Assuming you have staff, they will be expected to produce budget-to-actual financials to be reviewed by the committee. We recommend a minimum of quarterly reporting and reviewing.

The second is monitoring your organization's cash position to assure bills can be paid, funds are being put aside for a rainy day, etc. If you're a mature organization with a significant reserve or endowment, the Finance/Audit Committee will develop and monitor the policies for managing those funds. And, at a certain point, you may create a separate Investment Committee.

The third role is oversight. Beyond cash flow, reserve, and investment policies, your Finance/Audit Committee establishes a broader set of financial control policies and monitors their enforcement. It also oversees the annual audit process, approves the audit, presents it to the board, and, based on recommendations from the accountants, decides on policy changes.

There are two functions this committee is in a position to accomplish that are important to your fundraising work. The first is to provide a true and full cost analysis of all programs so that your organization solicits contributions that cover those costs. The second is to develop financial models for the future so that your organization can fundraise based on aspirational growth.

Staff will be integral to developing the documents and draft models the Finance/Audit Committee needs. But to the extent that these final reports and recommendations are those of your board members themselves, their fellow board members will more likely see themselves as a team working together to a particular end.

resource development

The Resource Development Committee works with staff to create a fundraising plan to be adopted by the board and then provides oversight for the implementation of the resource development strategy. But this is not only an oversight committee. It (or another group) is charged with leading and managing the process of soliciting your entire board for its annual contributions as well as working to engage your board in resource development. We will cover this further in Chapter 15.

governance/nominating/board development

The Governance/Nominating Committee, in addition to nominating and orienting new board members and renewing board member terms, has the responsibility of putting forth the slate of officers each year. This is one of the most strategic tasks, as the officers set the course for the board.

Even more important to fundraising, this committee is responsible for the bylaws and board job descriptions—ensuring they are being followed, reviewing them from time to time, and proposing amendments to them when necessary. These documents ensure that new board members join with a full understanding of their giving and fundraising responsibilities, and they serve as the basis for board member goal-setting and performance review. A sample board job description is available at askingmatters.com/boardresources.

program planning

The Program Planning Committee works with staff to develop and monitor program outcomes and provides oversight and guidance for strategic planning. Executive directors often prefer not to have this committee because the committee too frequently involves itself in operational detail.

The appropriate function of the Program Planning Committee is to work with staff to develop measures of program outcomes and to review programs from the point of view of mission impact, not operational implementation.

It's vital to fundraising that this committee continue to push for impacts. If this committee cannot clearly demonstrate the value of your programs, there is little hope your board members can make a strong case for support.

executive

As discussed above, the Executive Committee is essentially a management team. As a reminder, what your Executive Committee should not do is make decisions, except in emergencies when it's not feasible to bring your board together in time.

nine

recruitment

In looking to develop a board that will be engaged in its multiple roles—including, in this case, fundraising—it is important to develop an approach to recruitment that will lead to that result.

Potential candidates will inevitably be stronger in some areas than others, and you will, of course, be making judgments in each situation. However, unless you are clear on your ideal candidate, you cannot effectively evaluate the actual candidates you are considering.

As the Cheshire Cat said to Alice:

> **"If you don't know where you want to go,**
> **it doesn't much matter which path you take."**

There are six distinct criteria for board member recruitment:

1. Thought leadership skills
2. Access to resources
3. Willingness to make a personally significant gift and engage in fundraising
4. Ability to work as part of a team
5. Representation of different viewpoints
6. Deep personal concern for the mission

Every board member has some degree of all six attributes. Yet each board member will naturally be stronger in some areas than in others. While the work of the board, including the fundraising, is the work of individuals, the best result is obtained when there is an effective team. It is the team that motivates and supports the work of the members, and it is the collective distribution of the six attributes that produces the result.

the three thought leadership skills

ongoing basic

Ongoing basic thought leadership skills are the skills every organization always needs.

These include financial management, the ability to identify legal issues, insight into community needs and resources, knowledge about how to sustain and grow a business, expertise in communications and marketing, and human resources management. Each organization, depending on its mission and business structure, will need more or less of each of these skills.

- Which three of these basic thought leadership skills are most important to YOUR board on an ongoing basis? Are they well represented on your board currently?

ongoing specific

These are specific to your nonprofit and are ongoing needs. Some of these ongoing specific skills might be real estate development or management, union negotiations, investment management, subject matter expertise, or the representation of important constituencies.

- What are the thought leadership skills specific to your organization that you need on an ongoing basis, and how well are they represented on your board?

short-term specific

These are skills needed for a particular situation, such as a one-time purchase of a piece of real estate, or the merger of your organization with another. We often recommend not even placing someone on the board if the primary driver is this one skill, but rather asking the person to join (or lead) a special committee.

- What are some short-term thought leadership skills you need now or may need in the near future?

access to resources

Board members can bring a rich array of resources to an organization. They may represent companies that can supply gifts as well as goods and services, or know of other companies that can. They may know people who can bring their expertise to committee work. Or they may know other individuals who can provide in-kind services as experts or volunteers. Even providing space for meetings is a helpful resource.

Besides bringing critical resources to your organization, when your board members access these resources, they learn many of the skills needed to fundraise, they build relationships with donors, and they feel more vested because they've made a bigger impact.

willingness to make a personally significant gift and engage in fundraising

In Chapter 14 we will go into significant detail on what personally significant giving and strategic board member involvement in fundraising look like.

ability to work as part of a team

Teamwork, as we discussed earlier, is critical for boards. We've all had the experience of working with a "lone ranger." Lone rangers keep the board from coalescing as a team, and very few people make their best effort when the team is weak. Without teamwork, most board members will not fundraise. They won't sense that the board, as a whole, is embracing this role and won't take it on themselves.

A respect for teamwork is often hard to assess in an interview, so we've provided some sample interview questions at asking-matters.com/boardresources.

Part of working as a team is taking on leadership responsibil-

ities. Everyone on your board needs to be willing to lead something at some point—a committee, an event, or the board itself.
Leadership builds the buy-in, the perspective, and the deep understanding that give board members the confidence to go out
and fundraise.

representation of different viewpoints

What is needed to enable your board to consider the viewpoints of your various constituents?

The responsibility of board members is to the organization and
the mission, not to any specific constituency. However, board
members must represent the interests of all your constituencies—
and this means having a board sufficiently diverse that there are
members who, by virtue of background or life experience, have
the capacity to understand the needs and interests of your different constituencies.

Further, while it is not legally necessary that you have board
members who are actual members of every constituency (except
of course, where federal or state regulations require that there
be board members who represent client constituencies), it is critically important that your board strive for diversity, equity, and
inclusion.

While some have argued that this can compromise fundraising, it is our belief that it will actually enhance fundraising, as it
will strengthen the character and commitment of your board, and
the board together will be more motivated to fundraise.

DISCUSSION

- Have your entire board spend 15 minutes at your
  next board meeting making a complete list of the
  viewpoints that need to be represented on your
  board, and which of those viewpoints need direct
  representation.

---

deep personal concern for the mission

People should join your board because they're committed to
what you are trying to accomplish—because they have an emotional or deeply felt connection. That implies that the challenges or opportunities your organization addresses should be ones
that concern the candidate. Hopefully, the candidate would have
already demonstrated that concern and could explain in an interview why it is personally important to them.

Taking into account all six of these criteria for board member
recruitment, your first job is to figure out what's needed—in other
words, what's missing. Start with a wish list of what you'd like to
have on your board: skill sets, points of view, connections to resources, and more. This list will be part of your board prospectus.

board prospectus & job description

Recruitment starts with a board prospectus. This document is
like a recruitment announcement for a staff position—it promotes
your organization and describes the position generally.

It talks about what you have done, what you're trying to do
going forward, and how the board is critical to your work. We've

provided you with a sample board prospectus to customize for your organization at askingmatters.com/boardresources.

The second recruitment piece is the job description itself. No one can apply for any type of work without knowing what is required. The more detailed your job description, the more successful your board members will ultimately be. We've provided you a sample job description at askingmatters.com/boardresources.

Always keep in mind that you're not begging. You should only recruit board members who want to dig in deep and become truly vested in the achievement of your vision. If they don't really want to serve, getting them to do the hardest work—the fundraising—will be nearly impossible.

And you can't be shy about saying up front what will be required—in particular, your resource development expectations. Time and again we encounter boards full of well-intentioned people who had no idea what was expected of them because their interviewers soft-pedaled the responsibilities of board membership. As you'll see, our job description makes this abundantly clear.

There are two other items you'll need to prepare in order to begin recruiting. The first is a recruitment process. Who does the interviewing? How are decisions made? The second is a list of candidate interview questions to serve as a guide, which we have also provided for you at askingmatters.com/boardresources.

the process

The process starts with candidate identification, and there are three avenues here. Start by soliciting candidate recommendations from your Board and senior management based on the priorities identified in the prospectus. If program staff have contact with volunteers, include them as volunteers are already vested in what you do.

You may also interview or convene a meeting of key stakeholders and other supporters to identify potential candidates. A meeting has the added benefit of giving those who care deeply about your organization an opportunity to get to know each other, which deepens their relationship to your organization.

The third avenue is to conduct on-line and other research for candidates with identified qualities.

Once you have one or more candidates, obtain basic background material through the candidate or the referral source. If you have more candidates than slots, determine priorities among the potential candidates identified.

Schedule an individual meeting, between each candidate and a member of the Governance Committee, to assess potential interest and suitability. This meeting is the time to review the board job description to make sure the candidate is clear on their responsibilities, including fundraising.

You may, as a next step, invite candidates to observe a board meeting. You may also have candidates meet with additional board members and/or the executive director.

The last step is for the Governance Committee to make recommendations to the Board.

ten

orientation, assessment, and retention

orientation

Once you've voted to bring on a new board member, the orientation process can make or break that board member's experience. Keep in mind: most board members have never before been on boards, and they have no idea where to start.

In our experience, orientation is often a step that gets short-changed. Once a board member starts off on the wrong foot, it's much less likely he or she will become appropriately engaged.

Orientation is a multi-step process involving various meetings and connections with your new board member. We'll touch on five important steps:

- Staff/program orientation
- Review of board handbook
- Meeting with chair for committee assignment
- Board mentor connection
- Check-in plan

• staff/program orientation

The first step is an interview with your executive director for an overview of the organization and to answer any questions the new member might have about the organization. New board members also need to observe some programs in action and have an opportunity to speak with program leadership and staff.

- What are the key programs you think your new board members should experience in their first three months?

• review of board handbook

The Board Orientation Handbook contains the basic organizational documents that a board member should be familiar with. You'll find a list of the documents that could be contained in your handbook at askingmatters.com/boardresources.

There should be a meeting with each new board member to review the handbook and answer questions...don't expect they'll read it on their own! The meeting can be with a member of your Governance Committee or their board mentor, a position we'll talk about shortly. In some organizations, the meeting is with the board chair, but our preference is to distribute leadership responsibility whenever possible.

• chair/new board member meeting

Next is a meeting between your chair and your new board member to agree on a committee assignment. This is also an opportunity for the two of them to get to know each other.

It is our view that the chair, perhaps with guidance from the Governance Committee, will have an idea of where new board members are most needed and will best fit. The assignment should be suggested to new board members as early as possible, and no later than in the week following the new board member's first board meeting, as committee work is an important way for new members to become engaged and committed.

• mentorship

Each new board member should be assigned a current board member as a mentor. Mentors should meet with new board members to introduce them to the informal culture of your board and to be available to answer questions. They should check in regularly throughout the first year — at least quarterly — and make sure new board members are getting to know their peers.

• check-in plan

There should also be a more formal mid-year check-in meeting with the board chair or the head of the Governance Committee, to see how everything is working:

- Is the board member fully engaged?
- Do they understand their role and are they comfortable in it?
- Do they have any concerns about the organization?

If this sounds like a lot of work, it is. But new board members deserve and need this attention. They can't hit the ground running if they're not properly oriented, and that will also impede their ability to fundraise.

assessment

There are three separate assessments that need to take place each year:

- An annual individual board member assessment with a board chair, a member of the Governance Committee, or another board leader
- An annual overall board assessment survey
- An annual retreat to review the overall board assessment survey and set board and committee objectives

First, each board member needs to have a one-on-one individual assessment with a member of your board's leadership. We'll discuss this in Chapter 15.

The second is a survey that allows individual board members to evaluate how your board has performed as a whole. This survey should be anonymous and administered by your Governance Committee or an outside consultant, and the results should be discussed at your board retreat.

As we recommended earlier, your board should also hold a retreat every year. This is an important opportunity to review the results of the board assessment survey together and discuss how to improve the functioning of the board, in addition to being a time for your board to set priorities and major goals for the coming year and decide on committee objectives.

retention: term limits or not?

Some organizations have chosen a mechanical process to deal with the possibility of diminishing engagement by limiting the number of consecutive terms that board members can serve — generally two three-year terms. The downside of this approach is that

while it can provide a non-confrontational way to remove ineffec-
tive board members, it can also result in the loss of those who
are effective. We don't recommend throwing the baby out with the
bathwater!

The alternative is to engage in an active process of board member assessment so that the decision of whether to ask a board
member to serve an additional term is based on actual performance. Sample forms for the assessment process can be found at
askingmatters.com/boardresources.

eleven

---

engaging the board in fundraising

Once you've instituted solid governing practices and created a strong team of dedicated board members who are passionate about your organization and want to do all they can to fulfill its mission, it's time to involve them in strategic fundraising.

That's not to say it's easy—board fundraising is a challenge for most organizations. Board members come with a lot of resistance, have very little idea of what to do, and are often asked to do what's not in anyone's best interest.

Part of the challenge of fundraising stems from how the work is accomplished, as we discussed earlier. While governance is executed by the board as a whole, fundraising is executed by board members individually. This makes the work that much harder, and it won't happen without good management—or governance—of the process.

Further, just as a strong board is based on shared understandings, clear and accepted systems, teamwork, and more, strong giving and fundraising are based on the same.

For example, without creating mission moments and involving your board members in important decisions, they won't be motivated to give generously and help fundraise. But that's not enough. You also have to involve your board members in discussing—and coming to an agreement on—what strategic fundraising looks like and how it will happen.

personal financial contributions

To get to agreement on fundraising, you must first have agreement on the role personal contributions play in building your organization and fulfilling its mission.

Why is it important that the members of your board make personal financial contributions?

First, and perhaps most obviously, through their giving your board members provide important dollars. Your board members are most likely to give unrestricted dollars to be used where they're most needed, and they are most likely to give gifts that go straight to the bottom line—without event costs, for instance.

Second, when your board members contribute their own resources, they become investors in your organization. They have a bigger stake in your organization after they've contributed, and it is more important to them that it succeeds. The more significant their gift is for them, the more seriously they will view their work in your organization and the impact the organization is having. This concept holds true for board members of for-profit companies as well, as they are required to have stock in those companies.

Third, everyone looks to your board members to set the example. People generally expect board members to make many of the largest individual gifts to the organization. We all look at annual reports, donor rosters, donor walls, and such. We want to know what the board is doing for the organization.

Fourth, if board members are going to go out and ask others for their time and resources, those asks will be stronger if they make gifts themselves.

Fifth, today our institutional funders expect to see 100% board participation. This is considered basic best practices, and if you must report that only 80 or 90% of your board is contributing, you raise a red flag for foundations, corporations, and various government funders.

board fundraising

What are the goals of board fundraising? Why is it important for your board members to go out and help find resources for your organization?

The answers are very similar.

We ask board members to fundraise because it raises important dollars—dollars that can go right to the bottom line.

Fundraising further develops their sense of having made an investment in your organization. Fundraising is, as we've said, some of the most challenging work your board members will undertake.

It also sets an example for other volunteers to follow. For instance, why should your special events committee ask if your board doesn't ask?

Last, it impresses institutional funders that your board is committed enough to ask others.

tools for engagement

Ultimately, the goal is to maximize both personal contributions from board members and their fundraising.

However, if your board members are not legally required to contribute or to solicit contributions, how can you expect them to do so? It's not enough to inspire them through the best practices we've outlined. You need to specifically address the tools they need, set clear expectations, develop procedures, promote accountability, and more. Doing so is an important part of governance that often gets overlooked.

To do this, we recommend developing a five-part program to motivate and commit the board:

1. Make the Case: Why are individual contributions needed? What will your organization be able to do or not do with different levels of support?
2. Address Resistance: Why are your board members reluctant to solicit contributions? What can be done to overcome that reluctance?
3. Establish Expectations: Agree on personal giving and fundraising goals
4. Develop Individual Action Plans
5. Provide Training and Support

We'll cover all five steps in the ensuing chapters.

twelve

---

make the case
for fundraising

Telling your board that you "need" more money will not motivate their involvement. It's almost a given that you "need" more money, and continuously talking about need will eventually fall on deaf ears.

There must be a clear case that shows how much funding is needed, what it's needed for, and what it will accomplish. This is important for board members in motivating them to personally give, and in giving them the tools they need to cultivate and solicit gifts.

There are three steps to developing a strong case for support:
* Assign those responsible for identifying opportunities for growth
* Develop projections
* Create a board presentation and facilitate a discussion

assign committee members

The case should be developed by board members. Staff, of course, will provide critical information and direction, but it's up to board members to own it. When they own the case, it deepens their personal commitment and makes it much more likely they can persuade others.

Depending on your committee structure and the strength of your committees, the work might sit in one committee or might be delegated to multiple committees. Your Program Committee may develop growth scenarios and your Fundraising Committee will build projections. Or perhaps your Resource Development Committee will take the lead and ask various committees for input.
* Which committee(s) would develop the case at your organization?

develop projections

Whoever builds the case needs a schedule of revenue and expenses by source for the last three years so that they can better understand how the organization is sustained. Once they have the basic revenue information, they need to pull together projections for various budget scenarios.

Here are three general budget scenarios:

gap

This is generally the most conservative option. Here the goal is to sustain current programming by filling the gap between the full real cost to run your current operations and any committed revenue you already have for the coming year.

enhancement

The second option is a budget with short-term program growth or enhancements. It usually requires the board to up its game, perhaps in its own giving and almost always in its fundraising.

visionary

This budget helps fulfill the organization's long-range plan and vision. It is much more ambitious and requires broad, strong board support and involvement in developing resources.

	gap	enhancement	visionary
needed to run	$1,250,000	$1,250,000	$1,250,000
+desired to enhance		$150,000	
+desired to fulfill			$750,000
confirmed revenue	$1,150,000	$1,150,000	$1,150,000
gap to be raised	$100,000	$250,000	$850,000

create a presentation and
facilitate a discussion

Based on this analysis, the committee will then develop a presentation to the board to help them understand the importance of fundraising, especially soliciting individual contributions.

The presentation will include general statistics about the importance of individual fundraising to the nonprofit sector, such as those we provided earlier. And, of course, the committee will need to choose someone to lead the presentation and discussion.

Your board may decide to be conservative and go with the gap budget, or to push themselves to fund the enhancement or visionary budget. But whichever scenario they agree to, they will own it and be responsible for developing the needed resources.

thirteen

---

address resistance

Even if you have established goals and a board commitment to achieve them, and even if you have resource development expectations laid out in board prospectuses and job descriptions, there may still be some reluctance from board members to actually doing the necessary work of fundraising.

Since the work of cultivating individual donors and soliciting their support is not something most board members have experience with, their resistance is often based on three fears:

- Reciprocity: Anyone they ask will soon ask them in return
- Rejection: They will be rejected and feel hurt
- Damaging relationships: Asking will have a negative impact on their personal and business relationships

Unfortunately, much of this stems from what your board members may have been asked to do to date, which has probably felt like begging, arm-twisting, or "You scratch my back and I'll scratch yours." In addition to making your board members feel bad, it's not strategic—as virtually none of this develops long-term donors for the organization.

Therefore, the first step is focusing board members strategically. This means not asking them to hit up everyone they know or make gifts to their friends' organizations only for them to be asked to make gifts in return. These are not strategic gifts, as they're completely tied to your board members' relationships with the donors, not your organization's relationships with them...and this means that when your board members leave, these gifts will leave with them.

The goal is to cultivate long-term support—not just to obtain one-time gifts. The goal is to make fewer but better asks...to make friends, not sales.

DISCUSSION:

First, give board members the opportunity to openly express any concerns they have, and make a list of them on a flipchart. Then ask them to share their actual experiences in asking for or being asked for donations, and list those. They will notice that their concerns are generally not borne out in their own experiences.

Many board members fear that the process of soliciting support will harm a relationship. However, when we think of situations in which we have been asked, they almost always leave us feeling better about the person who made the ask. We respect their commitment. When your board members find the few people who could truly come to care about the organization and want to give, asking these people to do so deepens those relationships.

Once board members start limiting their asks to focus on building fewer, better relationships, they'll get beyond the fear of reciprocity. The ultimate goal—not only for board members but for the field—should be to eliminate quid-pro-quo fundraising, though we realize that is difficult to achieve given how ingrained this practice is in our nonprofit sector.

Strategic fundraising is also good governance, as it will inspire board members rather than burn them out as transactional fundraising does. How often has a board member said, "I don't have anyone else to ask...I've asked everyone I know and they're tired of hearing from me"? We've heard this countless times over the years.

Having said all this, organizations often shoot themselves in the foot by assuming that board members can just go out there and fundraise without training. Asking for gifts is not easy for most. It takes training and practice, which we will address in Chapter 16.

fourteen

---

establish
expectations

With your board members now committed to and more willing to raise money, it is important to create an agreed-upon set of expectations to which your board members will hold themselves and their fellow members responsible.

Establishing expectations is an important governance topic. Draft expectations can be developed by your Governance, Executive, or Fundraising Committee, or through a full board discussion with a strong facilitator.

Some boards ask their board members to contribute and

fundraise. Some give them the option to contribute or fundraise. Some have a minimum threshold. *We strongly believe the best policy is to ask everyone to make their best gift AND fundraise to the best of their ability.*

To explain our reasoning, we'd like to address the other options and the reality of each as we have seen it work with our clients.

give or get

Let's use as an example a "give or get" policy of $2,500. Each board member needs to give or get $2,500 for the organization. How does that unfold?

In one scenario, a board member with more capacity writes a check for $2,500, has easily fulfilled their give or get commitment, and has no need to do the heavier lifting that fundraising entails.

In a second scenario, the board member with more capacity very easily writes a $1,000 check and then gets three friends to each write a $500 check—very possibly in exchange for the board member writing three $500 checks to their own organizations. Both board members are now contributing the same amount, though they have different capacities, and the second board member is still doing the heavier lift.

Is either of these scenarios the scenario you want? Is any of these scenarios creating the motivating feeling we discussed in Chapter 4 where people on the board are partners with each other? Have equal skin in the game?

minimum gifts

Do we also discourage minimum gifts? We do. Let's talk about this, as many organizations set a minimum.

Unfortunately, what we find in case after case is that what you think you're setting as a floor for giving ends up being a ceiling.

First, if you set a minimum gift of some amount, most of your board members will give that gift without any other prompting or discussion. There's no reason to think others are giving more or that it's necessary to give more. To get past that challenge, you then would need to personally solicit everyone, at which point why not solicit each and every board member for a personally significant gift?

Second, minimums need to be set at a level most board members can meet fairly easily. Otherwise, there will be lots of resistance. This means the minimum is artificially low relative to the overall capacity of your board members. On top of that, you're still left having awkward discussions with the board members who have the most modest means, explaining to them that it's fine if they don't meet that minimum level. And that won't make them feel good either.

Third, a minimum gift can feel like dues, or a requirement, and runs counter to the idea of philanthropy. We want board members to give willingly and generously, neither of which is communicated through a minimum gift requirement.

personally significant gifts

We believe everyone on your board must give a personally significant gift, regardless of the other resources they bring to the table. When everyone gives significantly, it builds the team in addition to bringing important resources to the organization. So, what does personally significant mean?

"Personally significant" will mean different things to different people. Here are some of the descriptions we've heard over the years:

It's a gift that:

...I really have to think about

...is bigger than only one or two other gifts I make

...means I will not be able to do something for myself

...represents how committed I am to the organization

...feels like an investment

...goes beyond what I thought I could do

...I need to first discuss with my spouse or partner

...I can't even tell my spouse or partner about!

Are there exceptions? Yes, there could be, but only for legislatively mandated or other necessary representatives, such as elected officials. Even board members who are community or program representatives can make a gift that is "personally significant" for them, whatever the level. You must have 100% board participation in this.

DISCUSSION:

Break into groups of three and ask each group to come up with as many ways as they can to describe what makes a gift personally significant to them. Then ask the reverse question: What prompts you to make a personally significant gift?

How are these personal amounts set? Through the individual conversations, which we talked about in Chapter 11 and will talk about again in Chapter 15.

fundraising

As we noted earlier, a lot of the work board members are asked to do doesn't feel good and isn't strategic. Board members feel obligated to ask everyone they know for money. Some of their friends don't make a gift. Some, they feel, are not generous. Some friends turn around and ask them to make gifts in return. The effort feels fraught and burdensome.

This is not what we're talking about here. We're not talking about transactional fundraising—we're talking about relational fundraising. We're not making sales—we're enrolling people in our cause. Board members will be more comfortable engaging when the focus changes from "making the ask" to "making friends."

And that means the magic number is four:

- Four people to cultivate and solicit over time
- Four who would be truly interested in the cause
- Four who would develop a relationship that won't be 100% dependent on the board member and will survive the board member's eventual departure from the board

For a board member who doesn't have four of their own prospects, most organizations have plenty of prospects and current donors who need more cultivation.

We're talking about strategically helping the organization develop resources over time, primarily developing one-on-one relationships through in-person or other one-to-one meetings and regular communication, as these are most effective and need the assistance of the board.

Does this mean everyone will actually ask those four donors for gifts? No. Some board members will not be able to do it well, and no one should do a job poorly on behalf of your organization.

But every board member can build those relationships. Every board member can serve as an advocate and help cultivate relationships. They can...

- Invite a donor to join them for a visit to the organization
- Ask a donor to coffee to get to know them better
- Call or email a donor to update them on what's happening at the organization
- Personally thank a donor for their donation

Everyone can also ask for all the other resources that help your organization, such as volunteerism, in-kind products and services, or committee work. We find most board members are very willing to make these asks as they don't require the same level of confidence or asking skill that a cash gift requires.

While your board members might not sit down on their own to ask donors for gifts, they will likely join your executive director, development professional, board chair, or other representative to do so. When a board member is at the table and tells their story to a donor, it carries great weight even if the board member isn't making the actual ask.

special events and letter writing

There is no question that board members are more comfortable inviting people they know to a fundraising event or sending them a letter than they are sitting down face-to-face to cultivate or ask for gifts. With fundraising events, they can justify to themselves that their friends are getting a fun night out...or they simply support their friends' events in return. Letter writing is a bit indirect and low-key, as their friends can assume everyone got the same letter and it's not imperative to act on it. Yet both of these methods are often problematic board fundraising tools.

While fundraising events can provide visibility, or give you a means to honor people, as fundraising tools they are very time-consuming and expensive. People try to justify them as cultivation tools; yet in reality, very few fundraising event donors end up giving outside that event.

Board member letter writing to their "list" is also generally not strategic. Most of it results in small gifts, or ends up being quid-pro-quo fundraising, which doesn't benefit either organization.

Your goal should be to move your board members away from this as much as possible, and toward the more strategic long-range work of cultivating donor relationships that build a long-term, loyal donor base. Having everyone participates strategically is incredibly powerful and effective. A synergy is created that motivates people to do more. It builds leadership on the board and a deeper sense of commitment. It allows the organization to accomplish more than it possibly can when staff act alone.

fifteen

---

develop individual
action plans

We ask a lot of our board members. We ask them to show up at events, open doors, take on committee assignments, mentor other board members, make personally significant gifts, fundraise, host events, and more. Brian recently worked with an organization that had eleven ways board members could give during the year—everything from supporting three events to contributing an annual gift, paying board dues and more. And each of those opportunities to give was a separate request.

If you constantly ask your board members for help, it can start to feel endless to them. Just as they've finished one task or made one gift, they're asked for another. At what point will they have done their job? And if they know another request is likely on the way, will they make their best effort with the current one? Or say yes at all?

For your board members to do their best work, they need to have an action plan for the year. They need to understand what will be required of them in all ways so that they can see their work holistically and strategically. They need to be given the opportunity to think about the total personal giving they'd like to provide and how they can best allocate it to the organization's various requests.

This means sitting down annually with each board member to discuss everything from their own giving to how they will help fundraise to what other resources they can provide or track down, and more.

Not only does this process improve the resource development results of your board, but it also contributes to good governance as it develops a sense of teamwork and camaraderie that strengthens your board as a whole. Board members feel more responsible to each other and understand that this is a team effort, through which everyone is committing to their best efforts.

soliciting board member gifts

If best practice is to solicit all major donors in person, or at least through individual conversations, why would we not ask those who are often our most significant donors—our board members— the same way? Yet we constantly hear of a board chair who takes five minutes to solicit the whole board at a meeting, distributing pledge cards to be returned. Or one who sends a group email saying "It's time to make your commitments." That is certainly not the way to make board members feel important or to maximize their gifts.

Board members should solicit each other. It builds responsibility, strengthens relationships, develops leaders, and builds the team. It enables them to have frank peer-to-peer discussions. And leaving it to staff puts them in the awkward position of soliciting their bosses.

It's possible your board chair will take on the role of soliciting everyone themself, and there are benefits to your chair having conversations with each and every board member. However, that can be a lot of work if you have a board of 15 or more members. Therefore, we often recommend forming a committee, which not only spreads the work out, but enables several board members to have these rich discussions with their fellow board members.

Perhaps you have a standing committee that can commit to this. It could be your Governance Committee, since it's up to them to police board members who aren't fulfilling their job descriptions. It could be your Executive Committee, as they can learn invaluable lessons from these discussions that can help them run the board. Perhaps it's your Resource Development Committee. But it can also be an ad hoc committee.

The committee will review their fellow board members' past giving, look at other indicators, gather recommendations from staff, and then derive individual amounts to solicit. Committee members will each be charged with soliciting three or four fellow board members.

We want to underscore that the solicitation should be for an exact amount, just as it is for your other major donors. Each board member should be asked for a personally significant gift, with a discussion about what makes it personally significant, if warranted. That gift will often be a combined gift that includes all their various support for the year.

Keep in mind that the soliciting of board gifts should not be a year-long effort. It's best to have a tight timeline, early in your fiscal year.

resource development action plans

Either in conjunction with their being solicited or in a separate meeting, each board member needs to develop an individual resource development plan for the year. Resource development includes not only their fundraising, but all the other resources they will help develop, from in-kind products and services, to which board committee(s) they want to serve on, and more.

If separate from the solicitation discussion, this discussion can be led by a different board member and/or by a senior staff member.

Developing individual resource development action plans has many benefits. A plan:

- Helps everyone honestly and thoroughly evaluate the prior year. There's no point in moving forward until everyone agrees on what has transpired—both individually and as a board.
- Allows your organization to acknowledge all of your board members' contributions and efforts. Too often we don't stop to acknowledge all the great work our board members do.

- Reinforces the expectations of board membership.
- Helps board members identify all the ways they can make an impact in the coming year, and creates a mechanism through which they can be held accountable for what they agree to do.

sixteen

---

train your board

We see our board members as successful and confident in their lives—that's why we've chosen them to serve. Yet we can erroneously assume that means they can go out and fundraise for us right off the bat. Conversely, board members come to our boards assuming that fundraising means hitting up everyone they know, which, as we've discussed, is non-strategic fundraising, and causes them to join our boards with a lot of reticence about fundraising in general.

The truth is most board members don't know how to fundraise—certainly not in the way we really need their help. They may know how to send out invitations and letters and work on events, but when it comes to cultivating and soliciting individuals for gifts, they have no idea.

Let's not forget that most board members are sitting on their first board, and even if they've served on another board, they probably didn't do the work we're proposing...and almost certainly didn't get trained to do it.

- What percentage of your board members are sitting on their first or second board?
- What percentage of your board members have had at least five hours of fundraising training?

Good governance means not only training your board members about their legislative/oversight/fiduciary responsibilities, as we discussed in Chapter 5, but training your board to develop resources for your organization. Your board can't govern well without training on how to govern, and it can't fundraise well without fundraising training.

Let's not forget—we would never ask a board member to serve as a social worker in our mental health clinic without proper training, yet we ask our board members to go out and fundraise without any training and then expect them to excel. This doesn't make sense.

Your board members need training in many areas, perhaps none more so than in crafting their personal case for support. Most board members don't know what to say. They think they don't know enough about the organization to be articulate, and they need training to understand that it's much more about what they say from the heart than it is about knowing programs inside out.

They can start with the organization's case for support if that's easier, but then must personalize it to represent their experience and passion. They also need to be able to incorporate the stories of impact that they have developed by visiting programs and reporting back, and those they've heard from fellow board members.

Board members also need to learn how to reach out to set up meetings, how to deal with resistance to a meeting, how to ask rich questions, and more.

Keep in mind that training is an ongoing process. You can't bring someone in for a half-day training and assume that you're done. Your board members may have learned a fair amount. They may have practiced a bit. But they will need to learn and practice a lot more. This must be an ongoing process. That process might include an annual retreat, but just as important will be regular fundraising training and practice at board meetings.

- Is your board ready for training and willing to devote 4–5 hours to kick it off?
- If not, what are they ready for? Would they carve out 15 minutes at every board meeting for training and practice?

TRAINING EXERCISES:

Nothing is more important to fundraising than your board members' stories.
- At your next board meeting, break into groups of three
- Have each group member, in 1 minute or less, tell the others why they are so passionate about your organization
- Have everyone share what they liked most about each other's stories
- Repeat

Find other exercises at: askingmatters.com/boardresources

asking styles

One tool we recommend for your board is the Asking Styles, created by Asking Matters. The Asking Styles are driven by the concept that authenticity is key to building relationships, and building relationships is at the core of the fundraising you need your board members to do. When your board members understand their Asking Style and can appreciate all the strengths they bring to the table, they will be more comfortable, confident, and effective fundraisers.

The Asking Styles are based on two key characteristics; how we interact (extrovert/introvert) and how we think (analytic/intuitive):

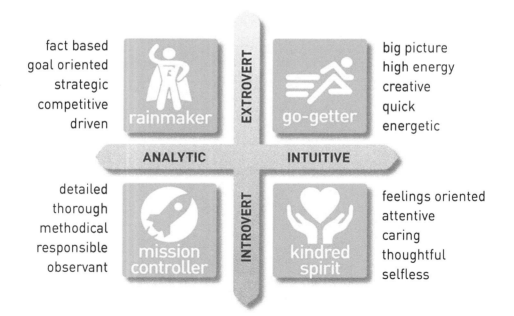

We encourage you to have every board member take the *free* **Asking Style Assessment** at **askingmatters.com**. It's 30 true/false questions take three minutes to answer, and your board members will see an immediate result in addition to getting further information by email.

Taking the Assessment will give board members a new perspective and more confidence. From there you can lead rich discussions on how to work together based on Asking Style, how to craft one's unique story based on Style, and more. We've provided you with several free resources, including exercises based on the Styles, at askingmatters.com/boardresources.

conclusion

We've been at this work a long time—a combined 80-plus years, in fact. And while so much has changed since we started in the nonprofit world, at least one thing hasn't: We human beings are still wired the same way. We want to matter. We want to be heard. We want to be part of the solution.

If you want your board members to care enough and feel responsible enough to go out and do the most challenging work—fundraising—they need to feel that they matter and have been heard. They need to feel they are an integral part of the solution.

When they are part of a collegial team that is fully engaged in strategic discussion, they will feel part of the solution and will do everything they can to make that solution a reality. They will give generously and help fundraise.

Getting your board to that point is not easy and it takes a concerted effort, but it's worth it. In our decades at this, we've seen the transformation happen again and again. We've seen organizations institute very strong governance practices that have allowed their boards to be incredible partners on every front, including fundraising.

This is our wish for you, whether you're a board chair who's trying to form the strongest team, or a committee chair or other board member trying to figure out how your efforts can make the biggest impact. Whether you're an executive director wanting to coach your leadership so you can work together as strategically as possible, or a development director looking for strong fundraising partners.

Whatever your role, we hope you've found some helpful guidance in our book that will help your organization fulfill its mission and make the biggest impact possible. Imagine that.

acknowledgments

Michael & Brian

We'd like to thank everyone who made this book possible. Huge thanks to Thomas West of Amarna Books and Media, without whom this book wouldn't exist. He's the rare combination of publisher, designer, editor, and sage. Many thanks to our super editor, Aliyah Baruchin, and to our insightful readers: Rob Acton, Gordon J. Campbell, Katherine DeFoyd, and Michael Seltzer. Their impact on this book has been tremendous. Last but not least, our thanks to all the board members and staff who do the heavy lifting every day. We applaud you.

Michael

I would like to thank the Board of Directors and the Members of Governance Matters whose advice and examples provided me with the understanding of Board dynamics that has been central to my practice. Their trust in my leadership has given me the confidence to develop solutions for the unique and challenging board assignments that have become my practice.

Similarly important in the development of my approach have been the nonprofit support institutions that have given me the opportunity to test my ideas with larger audiences, including: United Way of NYC, United Way of Western Connecticut, Association of Fundraising Professionals, Adelphi University, New York University, Baruch College, The Foundation Center, New York Lawyers for the Public Interest, The Foundation Center, The Support Center for Nonprofit Management, Nonprofit New York, Cause Strategy Partners, and many others.

Brian

I would like to thank Michael, first and foremost, for being an incredible mentor and teacher these past 20 years. Michael has taught me so much about board governance, which infuses all my consulting and training work.

Many thanks to my entire Asking Matters team: Jody Chromey, Michele Ericson-Stern, Kyle Nunes, Shannon Welch, Gary Ziffer, and Hannah Zollman. There is no Asking Matters without them.

A special thank you to all my clients, whose work with me has inspired and taught me along the way. I am so lucky to work in a field with such honorable people who strive every day to make the world a better place.

And always a thank you to my son, Richard, who serves as my guide star and who has lived up to his name.

other books from Asking Matters

If you've ever said to yourself "I'm not a fundraiser" or "I don't fit the stereotype," embracing your Asking Style will change your entire mindset. Once you understand your strengths—and challenges—you'll be comfortable, confident and effective. You'll have a roadmap for dealing with donors. You'll know what to say, how to conduct meetings, and how to close gifts.

For more than 30 years, Brian Saber has been helping nonprofit boards make the biggest impact they can. In his second book, Brian Saber uses the Asking Styles lens to help you build your board's strength. He'll help you understand how you and your fellow board members operate individually and collectively, what strengths you bring to the table, and how to employ those to best advantage.

CPSIA information can be obtained
at www.ICGtesting.com
Printed in the USA
BVHW021302141221
624032BV00025B/448